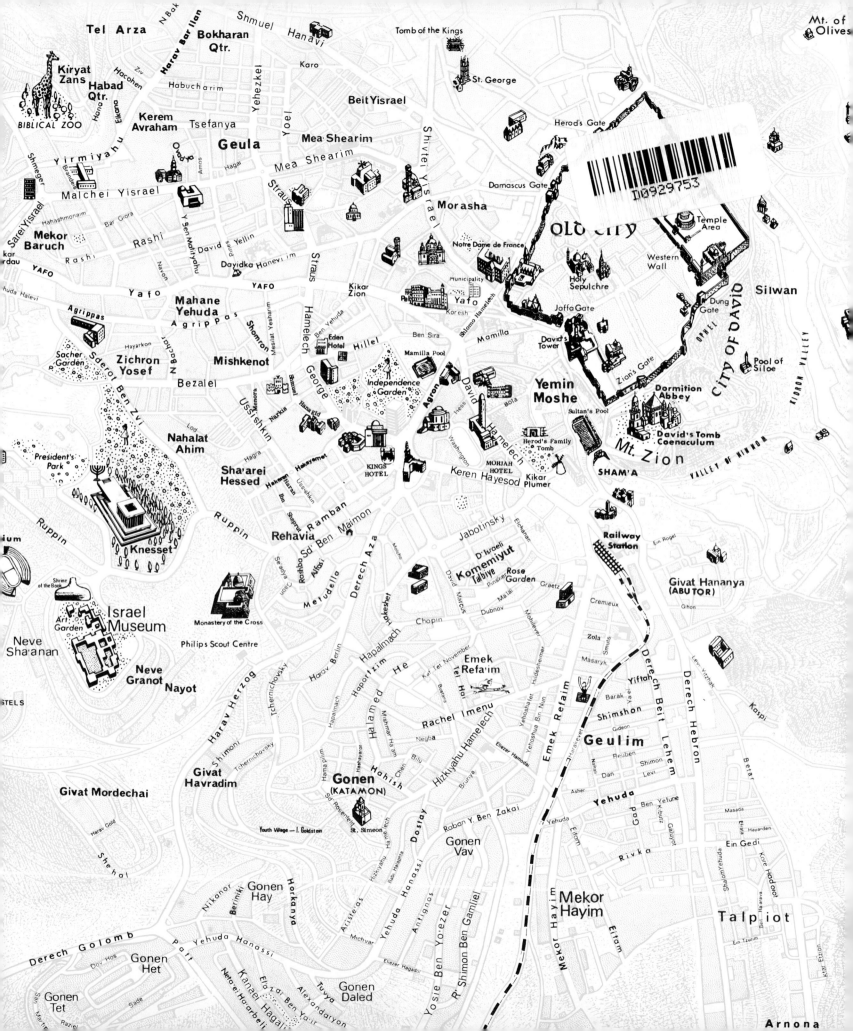

Library of Congress catalogue card 81-66418

ISBN 0-86710-004-4

© 1981, ARMON PUBLISHING, Jerusalem
and VILO PUBLISHERS, New-York

© All rights in the original hebrew works
are reserved by the authors

JERUSALEM
most fair of cities

Jaffa Gate.

VILO, New-York

In memory of Dr. Gershon Jagodnik

Photographs by :
Aliza Auerbach
Arielle Gibrat
David Harris
Michael Horton
Rosine Mazin
Zeev Radovan
David Rubinger

Nineteenth Century engravings
from private collection of the Editors.
The editors wish to express special thanks
to the Management of the Israel Museum.
See Watercolour by Turner (Joseph Mallord William)
from collection of the Israel Museum p. 18/19.
See also p. 39, 47, 121, 123.

JERUSALEM
most fair of cities

Essays, poems, legends
and Biblical quotations
edited by

Franklin Jagodnik

assisted by

Cécile Jagodnik
Hénia Stein

Foreword : Elie Wiesel
Introduction : Jacques Madaule
Essays by : Michel Riquet, s.j.
Roger Mehl
André Neher

"...כִּי בֵיתִי בֵּית־תְּפִלָּה יִקָּרֵא לְכָל הָעַמִּים"

ישעיה נו

...*for mine house shall be*
called an house of prayer
for all people

Isaiah 56:7

JERUSALEM : the face visible yet hidden, the sap and the blood of all that makes us live or renounce life. The spark flashing in the darkness, the murmur rustling through shouts of happiness and joy. A name, a secret. For the exiled, a prayer. For all others, a promise. Jerusalem : seventeen times destroyed yet never erased. The symbol of survival. Jerusalem : the city which miraculously transforms man into pilgrim ; no one can enter it and go away unchanged...

Here is the Valley of Jehoshaphat, where one day the nations will be judged. The Mount of Olives, where one day death will be vanquished. The citadel, the fortress of David, with its small turrets and golden domes where suns shatter and disappear. The Gate of Mercy, heavily bolted : let anyone other than the Messiah try to pass and the earth will shake to its foundations.

And higher than the surrounding mountains of Moab and Judea, here is Mount Moriah, which since the beginning of time has lured man in quest of faith and sacrifice. It was here that he first opened his eyes and saw the world that henceforth he would share with death ; it was here that, maddened by loneliness, he began speaking to his Creator and then to himself. It was here that his two sons, our forefathers, discovered that which links innocence to murder and fervor to malediction. It was here that the first believer erected an altar on which to make an offering of both his past and his future. It was here, with the building of the Temple, that man proved himself worthy of sanctifying space as God had sanctified time.

Elie Wiesel

THE UNITY OF JERUSALEM

Jacques Madaule

To talk of Jerusalem, of what Jerusalem means to a Christian, is difficult, and, strictly speaking, impossible. At best, each one can try to convey what it means to him, imperfect Christian, a Christian on his way towards a goal which he does not know whether he will ever reach. This pilgrimage, especially if it is a long pilgrimage like that to Jerusalem, is the physical manifestation of this march towards salvation. Since, for the Christian, Jerusalem is first the goal of a pilgrimage, the longest and most dangerous of the three great pilgrimages of ancient times : St-James of Compostello, Rome and Jerusalem. It ends by becoming, as we know, an armed pilgrimage. For the Crusades are nothing more than that. Later on, during the last century, illustrious travelers told of their wonderment and their disappointment.

For these two feelings had always existed, intimately intertwined, the one with the other, Jerusalem is for us -- and not only for us, I suppose -- the city of division, the city of partition. Its destiny is to assemble, but in the meanwhile it separates. Its division not so long ago, of waste lands furrowed by barbed wires, always seemed to me symbolic of its very destiny. Jews, Christians, Moslems (I enumerate them in chronological order and not in order of dignity) rub elbows there without merging and, especially, without loving each other. But if we want to consider Christians only, we see them here, as nowhere else, divided between Greeks and Latins, East and West. This goes back almost to the origins. It is Byzantium that had christianized Palestine before the Arab conquest. Byzantine basilicas and ascetic temples cropped up everywhere, and even in Jerusalem. One has to be really blind not to see that Eastern Christianity is at home here. The West was never more than an invader : first with arms, when the Crusaders refused to give back Antioch and Jerusalem to Bacileus of Constantinople, which had always been a part of his empire ; then with money, evidenced by the massive buildings of the monastic communities of the last century, the custodies a bit triumphant, even though Franciscan of the Holy Land.

It is then that Holy Russia, the third Rome, heir to Byzantium comes to the rescue of the Orientals. These facts, hidden

Model of the second temple (at the Holyland Hotel)

by many others since, date back to recent times, to the last century, and in Christian Jerusalem you can find their traces everywhere, but especially, of course, in the Basilica of the Holy Sepulchre, the supreme goal of the Christian pilgrimage, where the hours of the day are still divided into Greek and Latin. For many of the pilgrims who had come from the West, this was until not so long ago a permanent subject of scandal up until the day that the Pope and the Patriarch of Constantinople exchanged the kiss of peace.

I am not straying from the subject here : it is definitely about Jerusalem that I am speaking, of Jerusalem viewed by a Christian who has traveled there several times : first, at the time of the British mandate, then to the divided city and, finally, to the city reunited by Israel. It is there that I saw the immutable and the changing side by side. The immutable being the Old City surrounded by its pale Ottoman walls, with its three holy places : the esplanade of the Temple, the Mount Moriah, the traditional site of the sacrifice of Abraham, occupied for more than thirteen centuries by the Moslems ; the Wailing Wall, where the Jews pray and finally, the Holy Sepulchre. Islam dominates this landscape : the Ottoman walls and the Dome of the Rock are also Moslem. One would think that Judaism is flush with the ground and Christianity rather underground. It made such a strong impression on me, I recall, that this impression has survived all of my subsequent voyages. Though no conclusion can be drawn from this...

And then, all around, furrowed by ravines, the city of change, modern Jerusalem, which has again become, for the first time in nineteen centuries, the capital of an independent and sovereign state.

It is true, I am omitting the Latin kingdom of Jerusalem because, at that time, it was really a foreign institution of men camped on a soil that was not theirs, even though they did build some remarkable monuments on it. But still, the Franks or the Latins are the only ones, with the exception of the Jews, who ever made Jerusalem the capital of a state. I do not intend to get involved in political controversy here. Political controversy has nothing to do with my impressions, or with the fact that, for example, the sepulchre of Theodor Herzl, which dominates a hill of graves, that the relatively modest building which houses the Knesset, the Memorial of the Holocaust, Yad Vashem seem to me to add an essential dimension to the immutable Old City. Indeed there are two Jerusalems and, at the same time, there is only one. It is a living organism which breathes around the scars left behind by past times, but not so long ago.

That is perhaps what the average Christian who has come from the West misunderstands and finds disconcerting at first sight. What then did he come to venerate here? An empty tomb, that is to say a trail so obliterated that we can barely find a trace of a divine footprint on it. The concept of Incarnation, of God made man, is a specifically Christian concept. One cannot understand the Christian in Jerusalem if one does not try to put oneself in his place, if one does not try for a moment to believe in what he believes. This hilly landscape has not changed very much in the past twenty centuries, especially towards the East, towards what the ancient Hebrews called the Desert of Judaea and, beyond, the impassable barrier of the Mounts of Moab, which one sees so well from Mount Scopus. It is from this side that one climbs towards Bethany, towards this height which then descends into the Valley of Jordan. All this Christ saw, as we ourselves see it, with his « human » eye. This land that we tread, he trod with his own feet, and he breathed the same air of the heights that we ourselves breathe ; he was lighted by the same light. A landscape can change entirely, except for a certain quality of air and of light which one does not take along on the soles of one's shoes upon leaving one's homeland.

In Jerusalem as in Galilea, but totally differently, one encounters the Word incarnate, which is symbolized by the empty Tomb, because He rose to heaven, and also the pointed belfry atop the church of the Ascension on the summit of the Mount of Olives. One encounters the Word because one is in the same places where He passed. Across the same city one strives to follow, along the Via Dolorosa, the steps which led him from Pontius Pilate's praetorium to Golgotha. There the Incarnation becomes either present, or entirely unthinkable. Jerusalem, for a Christian, is a formidable test : that of his very faith.

That is why, most of the time, although frequently without admitting it, he prefers to look elsewhere, and it is generally with pleasure that he contemplates the picturesque oriental aspects of the Old City and even of the outlying neighborhoods that date back to the last century.

But if we try to approach Jerusalem in spirit and in truth,

Mosque of Omar on the ancient site of the temple.

then we become aware of an entirely different continuity in spite of ourselves. That is, without a doubt, what is demonstrated by the much discussed excavations of Prof. B. Mazar, which uncovered the Herodian pavement. So many things date back to Herod the Great ! In spite of everything, he is only one particularly monumental stage in the course of a very long history. It is towards the totality of this long history that we should strive at present if we want to be authentic pilgrims of Jerusalem. In reality, we are climbing towards Jerusalem. It is the Mountain of Judaea that rises over the Philistine plain. We aspire to it, we see it from afar, still unable to attain it, as it also happened to two very different pilgrims : the Spanish Jew Yehuda Halevy in the twelfth century and the King of France Saint Louis in the following century. Perhaps both traditions are legendary, but they excellently express, I believe, that which is inaccessible in Jerusalem.

And, finally, the strongest impression that I brought back from my stay up there in very different circumstances. The first time I visited Jerusalem was when it was a deeply divided city, lying idle on the surface under the surveillance of a foreign power, with sudden and bloody awakenings ; afterwards this division materialized to an extent : through the King David windows one contemplated, beyond no man's land, the inaccessible pale walls with their domes, their minarets and their belfries. I thought at the time of the City of Dis that Dante perceives on the other side of the insurmountable Styx, in the seventh canto of the *Inferno*. Finally, I saw it once again in another climate, reunited anew, but still varied and divided ; still the subject of tedious quarrels that the Christians have neither the right nor the possibility to arbitrate.

No doubt, it is because the city is varied and divided that we cannot attain it, that we cannot embrace it with one sole glance, nor the hills and ravines on which it rests, nor the centuries of its history. Neither the Christians nor the Moslems, no matter what importance they consecrate to it in their religious traditions, ever made a true capital of it -- whether religious or political. The Frankish kingdom was only a very small kingdom in the history of Christianity. Mecca, Damascus, Baghdad, these are the Arabo-Moslem capitals, Mecca and Medina, the holy places -- much more so than Jerusalem. For the Christians, the primacy indisput ably belongs to Rome ; Constantinople is the second Rome, Moscow, the third. But neither is comparable with Jerusalem. Jerusalem was never an imperial city, and it was never really royal except under David and the princes of his race, and later still under the Hasmoneans and the Herodians, the very ones whose pavements we discover today, that on which Christ trod.

Nevertheless, Jerusalem represents a primacy, a spiritual primogeniture. In Dante's cosmogony Jerusalem, as the summit of the Cross, is the center and in some respects the pole of a hemisphere, that of the emerging lands, whereas the other has the terrestrial paradise as a pole. It is therefore not around Rome that the world is ordered for Alighieri, but around Jerusalem. In the beginnings of the Church, it seems that special consideration was given to the Christian community of Jerusalem, those who were referred to as the Saints of Jerusalem and for whom collections were taken up in other churches.

What then is Jerusalem and what is its unique place in time and space ? I had honestly asked myself the question and I did not know the answer. There is not a city in the world that so totally eludes one. You can easily apprehend some of its aspects, and it certainly would not be difficult for me to enumerate them, to speak of the different neighborhoods, to extol the beauty of these stones of Judaea with which one builts its edifices ; to speak of my admiration for the new theater, that masterpiece that Israel built on the hills of Jerusalem ; to speak of its trees and of its flowers ; of its cemeteries so often desecrated ; of the deep valleys which surround it on the East and the South ; but Jerusalem passes beyond all this and overflows. Still, when all this and many more things will be said ; when we will have focused on people rather than objects, on those who pray at the Wailing Wall ; on those who pray in the mosques ; on those who pray in the churches and on those who do not pray at all, we would still not grasp the unity of Jerusalem, it would disperse itself through our fingers as it disperses itself in reality with long tentacles along its dry wilderness of the Mounts of Judaea, but more remains. And then there is Hebron, over there, with the patriarchs' graves, another holy city. What then is the unity and essence of Jerusalem ?

This is the question I posed to myself at great length and almost in anguish during the days and especially during the

The Mosque of Omar, left, and El Aqsa, right. The Western Wall in Ce

nights that I spent on this high place. What I can say, is that I sensed Haifa and Tel-Aviv living around me, but not Jerusalem because there are too many different things scattered over this high plain of Judaea.

Still, it is Jerusalem that one should understand in the end, Jerusalem and not Rome, Constantinople, Moscow, Paris or New York, if one wants to understand what is the true relation of a certain human community with a given space in a given time. I wrote elsewhere that Jerusalem is the city of resurrection. For us Christians, this is evident, for if we come here to venerate an empty tomb, we do it precisely because it is empty, because the corpse that was once inside it arose from among the dead. I borrow from the Orthodox liturgy, the oriental liturgy, this text which describes so well what the Holy Sepulchre, that is to say Jerusalem, represents for all Christians : « It is like the seed of life, and insofar as it is, in truth, more beautiful than paradise, more resplendent than any royal palace, that your tomb appeared to us, O Christ, the source of all resurrection. »

In the Talmud it is said that in each human body there is a mysterious bone from which that body will be reconstituted on the day of Resurrection. It was in expectation of this resurrection that so many pious Jews came to die there and to be buried in the Valley of Jehoshaphat that will witness the resurrection of the dead. Most of these graves were destroyed during the Jordanian occupation. But they were replaced by the Yad Vashem monument, where the names and the memories of the six million Jews massacred during the holocaust are preserved. Jerusalem is therefore more than ever before, for the Jews as well as the Christians, the city of the resurrection of the flesh, where all that is dead will relive. No wonder that certain of its aspects ressemble this plain of dried bones, that was shown one day to the prophet Ezekiel ? Is it not also the living image of its people, dispersed throughout many nations, speaking all languages, just as in Jerusalem one sees all styles of architecture, starting with the Hellenic period, and continuing through the Roman period, Byzantium and the Arab Orient up until modern day cement ? The unity here is invisible, it is all interior, and that is why, I was only able to sense it, but not see it, one evening at twilight, when the multiple, the living Jerusalem already enveloped itself in silence and was going to sink in the deep of the night.

Mount of Olives in background.

Jerusalem with the Walls
by William Turner.
Watercolour over pencil
touched with pen.
*Collection of the Israel Museum,
Jerusalem*

WEDGE ME INTO THE FISSURE

by YEHUDA KARNI

Wedge me into the fissure with each fallen stone.
Hammer me till I grow strong.
Perhaps I shall appease my land and atone
For the people's sin: the ruins unmended so long.

To be one of the stones of my city is all my desire.
Were my bones knitted in the wall, how glad I would be.
Is my body less than my soul, that through water and fire
Stayed by the people, who shrieked or went silently?

With the stones of Jerusalem wedge me into the wall.
Clothe me in mortar, and from
The very depths of the stones my bones shall call
Till the Messiah come.

At the sight of these stone-houses, enclosed in a stone-landscape, one asks oneself whether they are not the jumbled monuments of a graveyard in the middle of a desert.

Chateaubriand

A view of the Temple Mount and the Valley of Jehoshaphat. On foreground, the Jewish cemetery before 1967.

The Lord has laid the queen of cities low,
Its kings rejected, and its priests enchained.
God will have none of your appointed feasts.
O mighty cedar trees, burst into flames.
    Temples, collapse!
City, what hand has ravaged all your charms?
O that my eyes were as two founts of tears
    To weep for your mishaps!

                                        Racine

Ruins near Notre-Dame Monastery, before 1967.

THE LAMENTATIONS OF JEREMY

by JOHN DONNE

How sits this city, late most populous,
　　Thus solitary, and like a widow thus!
Amplest of nations, queen of provinces
　　She was, who now thus tributary is!

Still in the night she weeps, and her tears fall
　　Down by her cheeks along, and none of all
Her lovers comfort her; perfidiously
　　Her friends have dealt, and now are enemy.

Unto great bondage, and afflictions
　　Judah is captive led; those nations
With whom she dwells, no place of rest afford,
　　In straits she meets her persecutor's sword.

Empty are the gates of Sion, and her ways
　　Mourn, because none come to her solemn days.
Her priests do groan, her maids are comfortless,
　　And she's unto herself a bitterness.

Her foes are grown her head, and live at peace,
　　Because when her transgressions did increase,
The Lord struck her with sadness: th' enemy
　　Doth drive her children to captivity.

In this extraordinary desolateness, one must stop for a moment to contemplate even more extraordinary things. Among the ruins of Jerusalem, two kinds of independent peoples are able, because of their faith, to overcome the horror and the misery surrounding them : the Christian friars and nuns who live here and whom nothing, whether despoiling, maltreatment or the threat of death will force to abandon the tomb of Jesus Christ. Their hymns can be heard by day and by night in the vicinity of the Holy Sepulchre. Robbed in the morning by the Turkish Governor, they are back again at night at the foot of the Calvary, praying at the site where Christ suffered to redeem mankind. Their brow is serene ; their mouth is smiling. They welcome the stranger with joy. Without strength and without soldiers, they protect whole villages against iniquity. Driven by the stick and by the sword, women, children and herds take refuge in the cloisters of these recluse. What prevents the wicked and well-armed from pursuing their prey and from overthrowing these weak ramparts ? The charity of the monks ; they deprive themselves of everything to redeem their supplicants. Turks, Arabs, Greeks, Schismatic Christians, all seek the protection of a few poor friars unable to defend themselves. One has to admit with Bossuet that : « Hands raised towards the sky overcome more battalions than hands armed with javelins ».

As the New Jerusalem arises from the desert, in a blaze of light, set your eyes on the area between Mount Zion and the Temple ; look at this other small people living apart from the other inhabitants of the city. Held in contempt by everyone, they bow their heads without complaining ; suffering all kinds of vexations, they never cry out for justice ; accepting to be beaten and crushed, they don't even sigh ; when their heads are demanded, they hold them out to the scimitar. When a member of this outlawed community dies, his companions bury him stealthily, in the dead of night, in the Valley of Jehoshophat, in the shade of Solomon's Temple. If you enter the houses of these people, you will find them poverty-stricken, making their children read a mysterious book which these, in turn, will make their children read. This people still keeps on doing what it had been doing five thousand years ago. Seventeen times, it has witnessed the ruin of Jerusalem, but nothing can discourage it ; nothing can prevent it from turning its eyes toward Zion. When one sees the Jews dispersed throughout the earth, according to the word of God, one is

Byzantine niche called The "cradle of Jesus" in the Stables of Solomon.

undoubtedly surprised ; but to be stricken by a supernatural wonder, one has to rediscover them in Jerusalem ; one has to see these lawful masters of Judea, now slaves and strangers in their own country ; one has to see them waiting, despite every kind of oppression, for the King who is to free them. Crushed by the Cross, planted over their heads, that condemns them, hiding next to the Temple of which no stone is left standing, they persevere in their deplorable blindness. The Persians, the Greeks, the Romans have disappeared from the face of the earth ; and a small people, whose origins preceded those of these great nations, still goes on existing, among the ruins of its country, without mixing with the others. If there is something, among the nations, bearing a miraculous quality, we believe it to be found here. And what can be more wondrous, even in the eyes of a philosopher, than this encounter of the ancient and of the New Jerusalem at the foot of the Calvary : the first afflicted by the sight of the Sepulchre of the risen Christ, the second seeking consolation from the only tomb that will yield nothing at the end of time.

Chateaubriand

The Western Wall.

"IF, JERUSALEM, I EVER SHOULD FORGET THEE"

by HEINRICH HEINE

"If, Jerusalem, I ever
Should forget thee, to the roof
Of my mouth then cleave my tongue,
May my right hand lose its cunning."

In my head the words and music
Round and round keep humming,
*   ringing,*
And I seem to hear men's voices,
Men's deep voices singing psalms —

And of long and shadowy beards
I can also catch some glimpses —
Say, which phantom dream-begotten
Is Jehuda ben Halevy?

"If I forget thee, O Jerusalem" (Israel Museum).

Model of Jerusalem in Hasmonean and Herodian times in the gardens of the Holyland Hotel.

The memorial chamber of Yad V'shem.
Set into floor are names of the main Nazi
concentration camps.

THE DESTRUCTION OF THE TEMPLE

When the High Priest saw that the Temple was burning, he went up to the roof of the Sanctuary, accompanied by a platoon of apprentice Priests, carrying the keys of the Sanctuary.

They said to the Blessed Holy One:

"Master of the Universe! Seeing that we have not proved to be worthy custodians for You, let the Keys of Your House be herewith returned to You!"

And they hurled the keys upward.

A hand appeared and received the keys.

Aggadah

THE DESTRUCTION OF JERUSALEM BY TITUS

by LORD BYRON

From the last hill that looks on thy once holy dome
I beheld thee, oh Sion! when render'd to Rome:
'Twas thy last sun went down, and the flames of thy fall
Flash'd back on the last glance I gave to thy wall.

I look'd for thy temple, I look'd for my home,
And forgot for a moment my bondage to come;
I beheld but the death-fire that fed on thy fane,
And the fast-fetter'd hands that made vengeance in vain.

On many an eve, the high spot whence I gazed
Had reflected the last beam of day as it blazed;
While I stood on the height, and beheld the decline
Of the rays from the mountain that shone on thy shrine.

And now on that mountain I stood on that day,
But I mark'd not the twilight beam melting away;
Oh! would that the lightning had glared in its stead,
And the thunderbolt burst on the conqueror's head!

But the gods of the Pagan shall never profane
The shrine where Jehovah disdain'd not to reign;
And scatter'd and scorn'd as thy people may be,
Our worship, oh Father! is only for thee.

IN THE END OF DAYS

And it shall come to pass in the end of days,
that the mountain of the Lord's house
shall be established as the top of the mountains,
and shall be exalted above the hills;
and all nations shall flow unto it.

And many peoples shall go and say:
"Come ye, and let us go up
to the mountain of the Lord,
to the house of the God of Jacob;
and He will teach us of His ways,
and we will walk in His paths."

For out of Zion shall go forth the law,
and the word of the Lord from Jerusalem.

And He shall judge among the nations,
and shall decide for many peoples;
and they shall beat their swords into plowshares,
and their spears into pruning-hooks;
nation shall not lift up sword against nation,
neither shall they learn war any more.

Isaiah II

BY THE WATERS OF BABYLON

by HEINRICH HEINE

"By the Babylonish waters
We sat down and wept for Zion,
Hung our harps upon the willows —"
Dost remember the old song?

Dost remember the old tune
That begins so elegiac,
Groaning, humming like a kettle,
Humming, singing on the hearth?

Long — a thousand years already —
It has boiled in me — dark sorrow!
And time licks my wounds in passing
As the dog the boils of Job.

Dog, I thank thee for thy spittle —
But it merely cools and soothes me —
Only death can ever heal me,
And, alas! I am immortal!

Years, revolving, come and vanish;
To and fro the spool is humming
In the loom, and never resting;
What it weaves no weaver knows.

Years they come and years they vanish,
And the tears of men keep trickling,
Running earthward, and the earth
Sucks them in, in greedy silence.

MOST FAIR OF CITIES

by YEHUDA HALEVI

Most fair of cities, joy of the world,
    the great King's City blest!
To thee my soul is yearning
    from limits of the west.

Pity overflows within,
    thine ancient estate remembered
Thy glory which is exiled,
    and thy dwelling desolate.

O would that I might fly
    on eagles' wings, for I must
Rain with my tears
    till it mingles with thy dust!

I seek thee, though thy King
    is gone, and though instead
Of thy Gilead's balm are serpents
    poisonous and scorpions dread,

Yet shall I not, with tenderness,
    kiss thy stones at my feet,
And shall not the taste of thy soil on my lips
    be more than honey, sweet?

The Russian church and general view of the Old City

The Menorah, facing the Knesset.

I RETURN UNTO ZION

Thus saith the Lord:
I return unto Zion, and will dwell in the midst of Jerusalem;
*   and Jerusalem shall be called: the City of Truth;*
*   and the mountain of the Lord of Hosts:*
The holy mountain.

Thus saith the Lord of Hosts:
There shall yet old men and old women
*   sit in the broad places of Jerusalem,*
*   every man with his staff in his hand for every age.*
And the broad places of the city shall be full of boys and girls
*   playing in the broad places thereof.*

Zechariah 8 : 3–5

The Shrine of the Book and the Knesset (from the Israel Museum).

Jerusalem; Diary November 1898.

In the afternoon we were on the Mount of Olives.
Great moments. What couldn't be made of this countryside.
A city like Rome, and the Mount of Olives would furnish a
panorama like the Janiculum.

I would isolate the old city with its relics and pull out all
the regular traffic; only houses of worship and philanthropic
institutions would be allowed to remain inside the old walls.
And the wide ring of hillsides all around, which would turn
green under our hands, would be the location of a glorious
New Jerusalem. The most discriminating from every part of
the world would travel the road up to the Mount of Olives.
Tender care can turn Jerusalem into a jewel. Include everything sacred within the old walls, spread everything new round
about it.

Theodor   Herzl

הרצל

Herzl's tomb (Mount Herzl).

Here is Zion! Here is the Palace! Here is David's tomb! This is the site which inspired and delighted him, where he lived and was laid to rest: site twice holy to me whose soul was so often moved and whose mind so often delighted by the songs of the Psalmist.

Lamartine

The Citadel (view from the valley of Hinnom).

The northern corner of the Citadel, mistakenly called David's tower.

The city rising upon and resting on this wide and high plateau seems to be still glittering with the ancient splendour of its prophecies and to be waiting for the word that would let it emerge in all its radiance from seventeen successive ruins to become this "New Jerusalem rising from the Desert, in a blaze of light".

Lamartine

GLADDEN ME, O JERUSALEM

by YEHUDA KARNI

Gladden me again, that I may rejoice! Since I have grown
Out of thee, O Jerusalem, like a rose from stone.
Like a rose from stone, or like stone from an olive-treed wood,
or like, on lips of all the slain, a diamond of blood.
Gladden me greatly, for great is the grief of my cry
only salvation did raise me high:
since, whether I lay down to rest or rose, my bones
were bruised by holy stones.

The Art Garden of the Israel Museum.

The Shrine of the Book (Israel Museum) and the Knesset (Parliament) - from the air.

A SONG OF ASCENTS; OF DAVID

I rejoiced when they said unto me:
"Let us go unto the house of the Lord."
Our feet are standing
within thy gates, O Jerusalem;
Jerusalem, that art builded
as a city that is compact together;
whither the tribes went up, even the tribes of the Lord,
as a testimony unto Israel,
to give thanks unto the name of the Lord.
For there were set thrones for judgment,
the thrones of the house of David.

Pray for the peace of Jerusalem;
may they prosper that love thee.
Peace be within thy walls,
and prosperity within thy palaces.
For my brethren and companions' sakes,
I will now say: "Peace be within thee".
For the sake of the house of the Lord our God
I will seek thy good.

Psalms CXXII

FRESH IS THE AIR

by HAIM LENSKI

Fresh is the air when the storm is spent
And cloud after cloud has vanished into space.
A silence drenched with forest scent
Floats, purged of the dross of time and place.

Though darkness' shadow dims the whole world yet,
Already in the sky a patch of azure smiles.
The horizon slopes are split
By bursts of a rain that dwindles down the miles.

The Monastery of Saint John (near the village of Ein Karem).

Jerusalem has many names in Arabic : Urishalim (the Arabic form of Jerusalem) which is quite well known. But it is only in the Muslim tradition that the original name was pratically substituted by the attributive adjective AL-KUDS, the Holy City. For a short period, after his « hijra » from Mecca to Medina, the Prophet, like the jews, prayed in the direction of Jerusalem, though later on, he was mandated to turn towards the Arabs' worshipped place : Mecca. The Prophet's nocturnal miraculous journey (Isra) - at the beginning of the 17th Sura – would, according to tradition, bring him to Jerusalem. But many ancient commentators believe that that verse refers to the Prophet's ascension to heaven. However, the relationship between the nocturnal journey and Jerusalem has prevailed and according to a « hadith » recorded by AL-Zuhri, the Prophet indicated Mecca, Medina and Jerusalem as being cities of pilgrimage of equal worthiness. Nevertheless from at least one version of this « hadith », it appears that Jerusalem should have priority over the two other cities.

Caliphs and other Muslim leaders have embellished the Central Sanctuary of the Holy City, the Kubbat -al-sakhra (the Dome of the Rock) and the eloquent praise made by Makkadasi is still valid today : « At dawn, when sunlight illuminates the cupola, this edifice becomes a marvel to see. In the whole of Islam, I never saw anything equal to this ».

Ali Kamoun

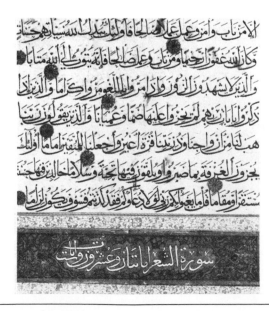

Page from the Quran
(L.A. Mayer Memorial :
Institute for Islamic art).

Worthy of praise is He Who took His servant by night from
the Sacred Mosque to the *Distant Mosque*, the precincts of which
We have blessed, that We might show him some of Our Signs.
Surely, it is He Who is the All-Hearing, the All-Seeing.

Koran. Soura 17:1

Holy Scriptures on the Dome of the Rock.

Fresco...

...and arcades of the Dome of the Rock.

The minbar, or pulpit,
brought to
the El-Aqsa Mosque.
by Saladin.

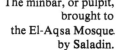

JERUSALEM 1961

by YEHUDA AMIHAI

On a rooftop of the Old City
there is a washing on a line
in a day's last light:
A white sheet of my enemy
a towel of my enemy
to wipe sweat from his forehead.

In the sky of the Old City
There is a kite.
But I cannot see the boy
holding it at the line's end.
because of the high wall.

We have many flags flying,
So have they,
to make us believe they
were happy,
to make them believe we were.

Rooftops in the Old City (Holy Sepulchre in back).

After these things, God tempted Abraham, and said to him: Abraham, Abraham. And he answered: Here I am. He said to him: Take thy only begotten son Isaac, whom thou lovest, and go into the land of vision: and there thou shalt offer him for an holocaust upon one of the mountains which I will shew thee.

Genesis, 22

Under the Dome of the Rock.

Inside the Old City.

The Sun by now o'er that horizon's rim
*   Was sinking, whose meridian circle stands*
*   With its mid-arch above Jerusalem...*

                              Dante

The old southern wall and the dome of the El-Aqsa Mosque.

Stained glass and ceramic tiles (Mosque of Omar).

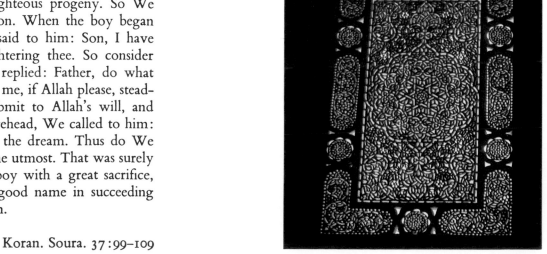

Abraham said: I am going to my Lord. He will surely guide me. He prayed: Lord, grant me righteous progeny. So We gave him glad tidings of a gentle son. When the boy began to run about with him, Abraham said to him: Son, I have seen in my dream that I am slaughtering thee. So consider what thou thinkest of it. The boy replied: Father, do what thou art commanded; thou wilt find me, if Allah please, stead-fast. When both were ready to submit to Allah's will, and he had thrown him down on his forehead, We called to him: Abraham, thou hast indeed fulfilled the dream. Thus do We reward those who do their duty to the utmost. That was surely a manifest trial. We ransomed the boy with a great sacrifice, and We preserved for Abraham a good name in succeeding generations. Peace be upon Abraham.

Koran. Soura. 37:99–109

Engraved door (El-Aqsa Mosque).

SPREAD YOUR WING

by H. N. BIALIK

Spread your wing to be my shelter.
Be my mother, sister, all.
Let my head nest in your bosom
And my prayers that vainly call.

Bend at dusk, the hour of pity,
My sorrows will confess the truth:
Youth exists here, so they tell me.
Where's my youth ?

I'll reveal another secret:
My soul burnt itself alive:
Love exists here, so they tell me.
What is love ?

There were stars, and they betrayed me.
There's no dream: there was before.
I have nothing left now, nothing,
Nothing more.

Spread your wing to be my shelter.
Be my mother, sister, all.
Let my head nest in your bosom
And my prayers that vainly call.

I WALK IN THE HOLY CITY

by JACOB DAVID KAMZON

I walk in the Holy City,
By pain and trembling tried,
As if a hidden wonder
Walked by my side —
And as I step on each stone
The voice of my heart I hear;
Gently ! Here once did tread
A seer.

Religious procession on the Via Dolorosa.

BEGINNING

by DAVID ROKEACH

The poem begins
from night that flows through the windmill on the way to Jerusalem.
From light on the spikes of stones
on the slope leading to the old well.
From thorns fom the fireflies between thorns.
From earth that yields up legacies of sorrow
for those who truly love.
From the moon who reads the symbols of the cards
in the palms of the tellers.
From silence harshening
in rooms behind curtains.
From summer echoing
behind a wall behind a curtain.
In realities of flesh and desire
and dream sprouting like grass
between roof tiles

Jerusalem, from the Latin Convent. Engraved by E. F. Finden, from a watercolour by William Turner (Private collection).

SACRIFICE
AND RECONCILIATION

Michel Riquet

Whatever his faith or his unbelief may be, there is not a man in the world, in this 20th century, who has not heard of Jerusalem. All around the planet, radios and televisions repeat its name to him or show him its image.

Hardly had the United Nations Organization been formed, when it applied itself to the task of giving the holy city of Jerusalem an international status.

Of all the books in the world, that which totals the greatest number of editions, translations and copies, the Bible of the Jews and of the Christians, Catholics, Orthodox or Protestants, recounts to the whole world, as it has to each generation for the past three thousand years, the history of the capital of the Jewish people which, although destroyed seventeen times, was never obliterated from history or from geography.

Today it stands more vast and more populated than ever, the new quarter encircling, like a case its jewel, the ancient city of King David, what remains of the Temple of Solomon reconstructed by Zerubbabel, then by Herod, and that which the Christians have added since the Emperor Constantine, and the Muslims since the Caliph Omar.

Like a rock, endlessly beaten by the storm, the holy city of Jerusalem withstands all of the hurricanes of history and, for a billion and a half believers, Jews, Christians or Moslems, it remains the center of attraction and the earthly support for their faith and their hopes, the marvelous symbol of a better world which they work hard at constructing or, at least, deserving. As is sung in the ancient Roman liturgy, it is of living stones, sculpted in the space and time of this world, that heavenly Jerusalem is built :

Ceolestis urbs Jerusalem,
Beata pacis visio,
Que celsa de viventibus
Saxis ad astra tolleris.

Jerusalem, heavenly city,
Blessed vision of peace
Which, constructed of living stones,
Raises its height up to the very stars.

How can one not admire such continuity, such a coherence of events bound to this corner of the earth, to this rock which, in the 7th century of our era, was capped by the cupola of that which we wrongly call the Mosque of Omar, but which the Arabs more rightly refer to as the Dome of the Rock, *Koubbat-al-Sakhra*

It is there, precisely, on this rocky peak of Mount Moriah, that this history began in which today the recent and most moving visit of Egyptian President Anwar el-Sadat, after so many others, has just been inscribed. He arrived on the day that the Muslim world celebrates the Feast of the Lamb, *l'aïd el kebir,* commemorating the sacrifice of Abraham, which both the Bible and the Koran situate precisely at the summit of Mount Moriah. Therefore, it is there that Abraham heard God say to him : « For because thou hast done this thing, and hast not withheld thy son, thine only son, that in blessing, I will bless thee, and in multiplying, I will multiply thy seed as the stars of heaven, and the sand which is upon the sea shore, and in thy seed shall all the nations of the world be blessed.» We note that this promise, inserted in the Scriptures, but even more so in the memory and the consciousness of the Jewish people, for more than three thousand years, continues to be realized. A billion and a half believers, Jews, Christians, and Muslims, consider Abraham, the believer, the father and the model of their faith. Was it not St. Paul who said to the Galatians : « Even as Abraham believed in God, and it was accounted to him for righteousness. Know ye therefore that they which are of faith, the same are the children of Abraham. » And in the Koran dictated to Muhammad one reads : follow « the religion of Abraham, the sound in faith, and not one of those who join gods with God ! Say ye : we believe in God, and that which hath been sent down to us, and that which hath been sent down to Abraham and Ismael and Isaac and Jacob and the tribes : and that which hath been given to Moses and to Jesus,

Via Dolorosa, arch of Ecce Homo.

and that which was given to the prophets from their Lord. No difference do we make between any of them : and to God are we (Moslems) resigned. » (Koran II, 136).

Is it not remarkable that it is precisely with this verse of the Koran that President Anwar el-Sadat had wished to conclude his pathetic appeal for peace and for the reconciliation of the children of Abraham, in front of the Israeli Parliament, the Knesset. To which the Israeli Prime Minister, Menachem Begin, responded with this citation from the Prophet Isaiah : « In that day will Israel be the third with Egypt and with Assyria, even a blessing in the midst of the land : Whom the Lord of hosts shall bless, saying, Blessed be Egypt my people, and Assyria the work of my hands, and Israel mine inheritance. »

So Jerusalem continues to be the city of encounters and reconciliations. It does not cease to evoke the dream of the prophets : « They shall beat their swords into plowshares, and their spears into pruninghooks : nation shall not lift up sword against nation, neither shall they learn war anymore. » (Isaiah 2 : 4).

The entire Jewish tradition, but also that of Christianity, attributes to Jerusalem a universal calling to assemble people in the same filial love of God and fraternal love of men. Sooner or later it should result in the advent of peace in justice and in law. But it shall always be at the price of sacrifice. This is what the rock in the heart of the Temple Mount reminds us. Not only did it serve as the altar for the sacrifice of Abraham, but Solomon built the altar of the holocausts on this base. During a thousand years, rams, lambs and bulls were immolated to atone for the sins of man to reconcile him with God until that day when Titus massacred the Jewish zealots who were fighting for their freedom there. But already, on another rock in the form of a skull, Golgotha, near the Temple of Solomon, another sacrifice occurred which, for the Christians, replaces all others, that of Jesus de Nazareth. In accepting his death on the cross, he reconciles men with God, the Jew with the non-Jew, to make of the one and the other the same and only people of God. As St. Paul says : « For he is our peace, who hath made both one, and hath broken down the middle wall of partition between us ; Having abolished in his flesh the enmity, even the law of commandments contained in ordinances ; for to make in himself of twain one new man, so making peace ; And that

The church of the Sanctuary of the Flagellation, marks the first Station on the way of the Cross.

And when they had led him away, they laid hold of a certain Simon of Cyrene, who was coming from the country, and upon him they laid the cross to carry behind Jesus. And there followed him a great multitude of the people, and of women who bewailed and lamented him. But Jesus turned towards them and said, 'Daughters of Jerusalem, weep not over me but weep over yourselves and over your children...'

St. Luke 23

Sixth Station of the Cross.

he might reconcile both unto God in one body by the cross, having slain the enmity thereby. » It is in Jerusalem, also, for the Christians, that this mystery of the death and of the resurrection of Christ by which the redemption of mankind and its reconciliation with God is accomplished. Even if Islamic faith interprets the event of the Calvary in a different manner from that of the Christians, it does not dispute its mysterious significance and also situates it in Jerusalem where it also situates the mystical ascension of its own Prophet Muhammad: « Worthy of praise is He who took his servant by night from the Sacred Mosque to the Distant Mosque, the precincts of which we have blessed ». (The Temple of Jerusalem, Koran 17). And it is towards Jerusalem that the prayer of the Prophet and his first disciples will be directed ; today it remains the third holy city of Islam.

Thus Jerusalem finds itself at the center of the religious consciousness of a large part of humanity, at the same time that it occupies a non-negligible place in the press releases and discussions of the United Nations. For the former and the latter, indeed, it is associated with hope ; a way to a vision of peace and a reconciliation of mankind.

As the psalmist sings :

« The princes of the people are gathered   together,
Even the people of the God of Abraham. » (Psalm 47,10).

The question is whether men will be capable of assuming the sacrifices and the indispensible renouncement of their individual or national egoism, to make of earthly Jerusalem, in anticipation of the one on high, the place of their reconciliation in a brotherly love open to all the people of the world.

Michel Riquet.

THE RESURRECTION

*And after the Sabbath, towards the
dawn of the first day of the week,
Mary Magdelene and the other Mary
came to see the Sepulchre. And behold
there was a great earthquake, for an
angel of the Lord came down from heaven,
and drawing near rolled away the stone
and sat thereon. His appearance was as
lightning and his raiment white as snow.
And for fear of him the guards quaked, and became
as dead men.*

*But the angel answered and said to the
Women, "Fear not ye, for I know that ye
seek Jesus, who was crucified. He is not
here, for he is risen, even as he said come
behold the place where he lay. And go ye
quickly and tell his disciples that he is risen from
the dead."*

St. Matthew 28

Frescoes, Dome and rock of the Agony (Basilica of the Agony) 1, 2, 3,
Altar and Latin chapel on the site of the crucifixion (Tenth and Eleventh Station of the Cross) 4,

*And he bore me away in spirit to a
great and high mountain, and he showed me
the holy city Jerusalem, coming down from
heaven, in the glory of God. The radiance
thereof was like to a stone most precious, to
a jasper stone, crystal clear. It had a great and
high wall, with twelve gates: at the twelve gates
were twelve angels, and names were inscribed
thereon, the names of the twelve tribes of
Israel. On the east were three gates; and on
the north, three gates and on the south, three
gates; and on the west, three gates. And the
wall of the city had twelve foundation stones,
and on them were the twelve names of the
twelve apostles of the Lamb.*

Apocalypse, 21

In the church of the Nativity — Bethleem.

SYMBOLIC SIGNIFICANCE OF JERUSALEM

A protestant viewpoint

Roger Mehl

Like all of the places in the Holy Land, like all of the places described in biblical tradition, Jerusalem holds an important place in the hearts of Protestants. From their earliest years, in Sunday school, they learn about the geography of Palestine and the topography of Jerusalem. This city where their Lord rose to celebrate Easter, and where he endured the punishment of the crucifixion, is a part of their individual and collective memory. In their eyes, as in the eyes of all Christians, the revelation of God is neither intemporal nor abstract : at a precise moment in history, in a precise place on earth, the Eternal God saw fit to manifest himself in the person of Jesus Christ. Christian faith is thus linked to a specific time and place. The well-known Protestant missionary and ethnologist Maurice Leenhardt recounts that the great difficulty he encountered in evangelizing the Kanaka people was to convince his listeners that Jerusalem was a real place, that by taking a boat and leaving their city they would really find a land similar to their own, Palestine, where they could disembark and walk towards Jerusalem. By means of this example, one can measure the entire distance that separates the mythical consciousness from the historical consciousness. Christianity, instead of referring us back to a time beyond all time and to a place which is, in the literal sense of the word, a utopia, refers us back to a precise and datable moment in history and to a geographically determinable place. This time and this place participate in the uniqueness of events that occurred « when Cyrenius was governor of Syria » (Luke 2:2), or again « under Pontius Pilate ».

The Protestants cannot express their faith without referring to Jerusalem. They like to go and visit the holy places, while all the time regretting that they have been so disfigured by the buildings constructed by a well-meaning but unintelligent piety. They prefer, without a doubt, the sites and monuments

Bethany by A. Willmore.

that bear witness to the history of the chosen people and which have been better preserved, or the landscapes -- frequently desert -like -- which evoke the wanderings of the Lord across his Land.

They use, like everyone, the sanctioned expressions of « the Holy Land », the « holy places ». But I suspect that they do not accord the same weight to the adjective « holy » as do other Christian faiths. In the real meaning of the word, only one is holy, the trinitarian God. It is He who sanctifies, but He sanctifies the heart of man, the community of the faithful, not objects and places. Objects and places are there to remind us that the great creation of God was not accomplished in some metaphysical heaven, but, of course, here on earth. Objects and places, no matter how moving they can be by the memories that they evoke, cannot be the foundation of any faith. The idea of a pilgrimage to Jerusalem, if this word means something other than a voyage to try to have a more concrete knowledge of the places described in the Scriptures and to acquire a better understanding of them, is foreign to the Protestant mentality. The Reformers of the 16th century certainly shared with their contemporaries the conviction that it was necessary to stop the Turkish invasion, a peril for Christianity, but they did not consider liberating the holy places as a major task for the Church. They were deeply convinced that the full meaning of the revelation of God in Christ was accessible to the believer through the Scriptures and the « living sermon » (Calvin) of the Gospel.

The Protestants are convinced, as well, that faith is not linked, is no longer linked since the Coming of Christ, to specific places. They remember the conversation that Jesus had with the Samaritan. She states : « Our fathers worshipped in this mountain and ye say, that in Jerusalem is the place where men ought to worship », and Jesus answers : « Woman, believe me the hour cometh, when ye shall neither in this mountain, nor yet at Jerusalem, worship the Father. Ye worship ye know not what : we know what we worship : for salvation is of the Jews. But the hour cometh, and now is when the true worshippers shall worship the Father in spirit and in truth. » (John 4:21-23). This is a very significant passage : on the one hand it affirms the independence of faith from places, on the other hand it affirms, no less firmly, the idea that salvation does not enter the world by means of a flashing intuition but through the history of a people.

Protestant piety has always attached more importance to history than to a space. The knowledge of the history of salvation predominates over the knowledge of places. The latter is only a complement of the former.

To make the knowledge of the places where the Jewish people and Jesus had lived a condition for the access to faith, would be in the eyes of the Protestants to forget that, as apostle St. Paul reminds us, henceforth we no longer know Christ in the human sense, after the flesh (II Corinthians 5:16), it would be repeating the error of the women who sought him in his tomb ; because if the Christian faith cannot forget that the word was made flesh, as is recounted in the Prologue to John, it should no longer search for Christ where he is not, but in the glory of his Resurrection. Therefore, by meditating on the Scriptures, a humble believer who has never left his village can know Christ as well as the one who has traveled the roads of Palestine and the streets of the Old City of Jerusalem, either as a tourist, an archaeologist, or even as a pious man.

These theological statements are necessary to better situate the Protestant attitude with regard to Jerusalem. The Protestant churches have always abstained from taking part in the quarrel concerning the holy places which has so frequently in the past produced regrettable confrontations among Christian churches, and which continues to do so.

The history of the revelation of God is closed as far as the Protestants are concerned. The events of the History of Jesus, inseparable from the history of the Jewish people, are events which have a unique value ; they will never be repeated. Space is the place of repetition, that is why it is less important than time, which is the place of universality.

But this being said, in the eyes of the Protestants Jerusalem remains a precious memorial, a city which should be preserved because it is forever linked to the unique events that occurred there two thousand years ago. When a Protestant speaks of Jerusalem, he does so with a much greater respect than when he speaks of any other city, no matter how prestigious it may be. The most glorious memories fade besides this memory of a modest evangelical event. As the living reminder of this memory, Jerusalem appears like a symbolic city. If this memory is other than something acquired from a book or sentimental, why shouldn't Jerusalem be the symbol of the reconciliation of peoples. Jerusalem, the city

A view of the Temple Mount.

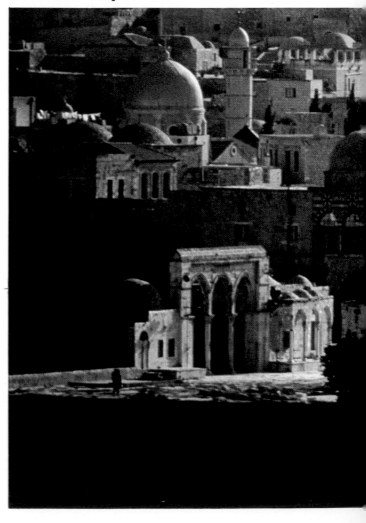

which kills prophets, is also the city where the Church first appeared, founded upon the reconciliation of men with God and men amongst themselves. More than Rome and more than Geneva, Jerusalem finds in its past the justification for a vocation. When the Pope and the patriarch of Constantinople met in Jerusalem, the Protestants applauded this meeting, seeing in this meeting the sign and the announcement of a great reconciliation of the Churches of Christ. But they need not shut themselves off in the sole search for their unity. Or rather this unity will not be fully meaningful unless it also contributes to the unity of the human race, to the reconciliation of Christians and Jews, of Jews and Muslims.

I stressed the reasons why the Protestants were not very interested in the quarrel concerning holy places. They do not expect that the care or the responsibility for such and such a part of the holy places will be entrusted to them. They are, without a doubt, very divided politically with respect to the form that the solution to the conflict between Israel and the Arabs should take. They are, doubtless, unanimous, as the Ecumenical Council of Churches has frequently declared, in wanting the people of Israel to enjoy a peaceful and secure existence. The diversities naturally appear in the choice of solutions to arrive at this end. But could not the presence in Jerusalem of most of the Christian communities be, in the future, an element of peace ? These communities certainly will not lay claim to the rights of possession. But they can rightfully take part in all of the solutions enabling free access to the holy places for all. Without calling into question the undeniable seniority of the rights of Israel, perhaps the Christian churches, at a given moment, could play a modest role of mediator between the partners. The Protestant churches, if it were simply a matter of free access and free encounter, and not of the possession of the holy places, would surely not remain indifferent to a process which would contribute to bringing to the attention of the entire world the symbolic meaning of the city of Jerusalem. For the Protestants, Jerusalem would not become for all that, in the strong meaning of the word, a holy city, but – and this would be even more beautiful – a city sanctified by the spirit of peace

JERUSALEM 1967

by YEHUDA AMICHAI

Jerusalem port city on the shores of eternity.
The Holy Mount is a huge ship, a luxurious pleasure
craft. From the lattices of her Western Wall happy
saints look out, travellers. Chassidim on the dock wave
goodbye, shout hurrah till we meet again. She's
always arriving, always sailing. And the gates and the docks
and the policemen and the flags and the high masts of churches
and mosques and the smokestacks of synagogues and the boats
of praise and waves of mountains. The voice of the ram's horn is
*   heard: still*
another sailed. Day of atonement sailors in white uniforms
climb among ladders and ropes of tested prayers.

And the trade and the gates and the gold domes:
Jerusalem is the Venice of God.

Holy domes in Jerusalem.

Greek chapel of the calvary. (Twelfth Station inside the Holy Sepulchre).

... These olive-trees are among the thickest I have ever encountered: according to tradition, they go back to the memorable day of the agony of the God-man who chose to hide his divine anxieties among them. Their appearance would corroborate, if need be, the traditional reverence they are held in. Their tremendous roots have lifted the earth and the stones covering them several feet above the ground, presenting the pilgrim with natural seats on which he may kneel or sit down to be penetrated by the pious thoughts descending from their silent crowns. Gnarled, fluted trunks, furrowed by age, rise like powerful columns wavering from right to left, as if stricken in years; their huge, intertwined boughs, pruned a hundred times to rejuvenate them, are bent towards the ground. These old and heavy boughs bear younger branches rising towards the sky and a few stems only a year or two old, crowned by bunches of leaves and blackened by small blue olives that fall like heavenly relics at the feet of the Christian traveller.

Lamartine

Garden of Gethsemane.

THE OLIVE TREE

by NATHAN ALTERMAN

Summer has reigned
Seventy years;
Its mornings have poisoned with avenging light.
The Olive tree alone,
My abandoned brother,
Has not withdrawn in battle from their brightness.

How holy is its vow, for its black branches
Bear neither star nor moon.
Only its poverty, like the Song of Songs, O Earth,
Pierces the heart of your stones.

Perhaps from the eyes of its god, its lord,
One tear is granted, heavy and hot,
When like a bookkeeper, breathing anger,
He crouches lonely over your book.

When you wish your mountains to die
And herds bleat for rain and fodder,
It will stand watch on the wall, your solitary bridegroom,
And you will know your life is in its keeping.

And in the evening bleeding with the sunset
It will feel along your face — "Where are you?..."
In its twisted trunk, in the fire of its veins,
It keeps and preserves your tears.

When from the distance the red desert wind
Springs violently forth,
It will withdraw
In terror,
For the mountain shall not fall, its heart shall not grow still
So long as one sapling
Tears forth from its side.

HOLY GRANDMOTHERS IN JERUSALEM

by ESTHER RAAB

Holy grandmothers in Jerusalem
May your virtue protect me.
The smell of blossoms and blooming orchards
I suckled with my mother's milk.
Feet soft as hands, fumbling
In the torrid sand,
And tousled eucalypti
Laden with bees and hornets
Whispered a lullaby to me.
Seven times shall I steep myself
Into the Mediterranean
To prepare for King David, my beloved,
And I shall go up to him, with glorious dignity,
To the mountains of Jerusalem;
I shall sit with Deborah under the date-tree,
Have coffee with her and talk
About war and defence.
Holy grandmothers in Jerusalem,
May your virtue protect me.
I can feel the smell of your garments,
The aroma of Sabbath-candles and naphtaline.

PRAYER

by *AVRAHAM SHLONSKY*

... Forgive me, You, whom we called by name,
Forgive my words, my confused spirit too.
I am not to blame, I am not to blame —
Teach me to bleat to Your creatures like You.

Notes of supplication in the stones of the Western Wall.

*Our feet are standing
within thy gates, O Jerusalem;
Jerusalem, that art builded
as a city that is compact together.*

Psalms CXXII : 2–3

The gates of the Old City.

JERUSALEM 1967

by YEHUDA AMICHAI

I and Jerusalem like blindman and cripple.
She sees for me
Until the Dead Sea, until the end of days.
And I hoist her on my shoulders
And walk blind in my darkness beneath.

*And when the queen of Saba saw all the wisdom of Solomon, and
the house which he had built, and the meat of his table, and
the apartments of his servants, and the order of his ministers,
and their apparel, and the cupbearers, and the holocausts, which
he offered in the house of the Lord: she had no longer any
spirit in her,*

*And she said to the king: The report is true, which I heard
in my own country, of thy words, and of thy wisdom.*

Kings ii, 10 : 6

*And King Solomon gave the queen of Saba all that she desired,
and asked of him; besides what he offered her of himself
of his royal bounty. And she returned, and went to her own
country with her servants.*

Kings ii, 10 : 13

Ethiopian Church

An Ethiopian Orthodox priest.

GOD LIVES!

by I. Z. RIMON

God lives! The splendour of the skies says so,
And the black storm that hides them also speaks;
God lives! The ornament of earth says so,
And the tempest uprooting forest also speaks;
God lives! The day in its brilliance says so,
And the night with its terror also speaks;
God lives! The purity of river says so,
And the heavy burden of fog also speaks;
God lives! The rich crop of mountain says so,
And the gushing flow of lava also speaks;
God lives! Life in its spring says so,
And death that is cruel also speaks;
God lives! The sea in frothing waves says so,
And in its whispered yearnings also speaks;
God lives! My heart, alien but bursting, says so,
And flowing into God's lap also speaks.

HEAVENLY JERUSALEM,
JERUSALEM OF THE EARTH

by LEA GOLDBERG

Divide your bread in two,
Heavenly Jerusalem, Jerusalem of the Earth,
Jewel of thorn on your slopes
And your sun among the thistles.
A hundred deaths rather than your mercy!
Divide your bread in two,
One half for the fowls of the sky;
The other,
For heavy feet to trample
At the crossroads.

People are walking in the counterfeit city
Whose heavens pass like shadows,
And no one trembles.
Sloping lanes conceal
The greatness of her past.

The children of the poor
Sing with indifferent voices:
'David, King of Israel, lives and is'."

Over my house
One late swallow.
All the other swallows
Have already returned to the north.

Over my head
Towards evening,
In a city
Weary of wanderings
In a city of wanderers,
Small, trembling wings
Trace circles of despair.

A sky of Hebron glass.
The first lamp of night.
Swallow with no rest.
Arrested flight.

What now?

JERUSALEM

by *YAAKOV FICHMAN*

Jerusalem! Cry of the hungry heart, oblivion's
garden beyond the hills when refugees fled the storm —
Silence you are, submission and rebellion.
Because of you, heart shudders, the griefs swarm.

By green of your earth I swear and by your sunlight.
I inherit the desolation that remains.
I stand like a tree in stone, by you spellbound —
Soul woven with soul, my root in your dry veins.

I love what survives in you as cold lava,
The rejoicing sound of ancient days,
Echoing still from your white rocks of silence.

But with your holiness is now my strife,
And I have come to smash rocks into clods.
Dead splendour rests on furrows of new life.

An old courtyard.

WELCOME, QUEEN SABBATH

by ZALMAN SCHNEOUR

Oh, come let us welcome sweet
Sabbath the Queen!

The cobbler abandoned his awl and his thread,
The tailor's brisk needle now sleeps in its bed.
Father has bathed, washed his hair, and he says:
Sweet Sabbath is near,
Sweet Sabbath is here,
Oh, come let us welcome sweet Sabbath the Queen!

The storekeeper locked and bolted his store,
The teamster unbridled his horse at the door,
The sexton runs hither and thither and says;
The sun sets in the sky,
Sweet Sabbath is nigh,
Oh, come let us welcome sweet Sabbath the Queen!

The white-bearded cantor has hastened along
To welcome the Sabbath with blessing and song,
Dear mother is lighting the candles and prays:
Day of holiness, rest,
Forever be blest,
Oh, come let us welcome sweet Sabbath the Queen!

Friday night : on the way to the Western Wall.

SIMHAT TORAH

by *JUDAH LEIB GORDON*

Lehayyim, my brethren, Lehayyim, I say,
Health, peace, and good fortune I wish you to-day.
To-day we have ended the Torah once more;
To-day we begin it anew, as of yore.
Be thankful and glad and the Lord extol,
Who gave us the Law on its parchment scroll.

The stained glass windows by Chagall in the modern synagogue of the Hadassah Hospital.

from HAGIGAT KAYITZ

by NATHAN ALTERMAN

... The city's a city. Although it's clear that there are times
when the city's a person, the person — time, and time — summer.
In general, they interchange and there's no hammer made
Can nail them down to stay. One thing cannot be denied,
Without symbols and metaphors you can't have poetry,
And though a green tree shrugs its shoulders outside,
It too is delighted when a fresh simile
Or symbol rouses it like rain from heaven.
— There's lots of interest in metaphors. But even there you mustn't
*   exaggerate.*
The more you do, the more you make.
Things fall into temper, and they take to their legs and scamper away...

A view of the modern City, with the old City in the background.

SONG OF THE SNOW

by *ZALMAN SCHNEOUR*

Oh, who crumbles up the heavens!
Here they fall in crumbs, in crumbs,
And the streets are merged — Be blessed
Who makes the changing seasons come!

There were fields — tell us where?
There were gardens — where are they?
Everything is white, white,
All colors hide themselves away.

Laughter, snow on every face
Shadows — the sleighs go past;
In confusion of pure feathers
Melting are the steeple tops.

Snow is swirling — in his dance
Swept away is one black bird;
Kra-Kra-Kra... Oh raven, raven,
Everything is pure, is pure!...

For out of Zion shall go forth the law,
and the word of the Lord from Jerusalem.

Isaiah II

Torah scribe.

JERUSALEM 1968

by DAVID ROKEACH

I

You want to know the number of gates
in Jerusalem. I count seven gates open
to you, four barred to me,
a golden gate for the lingering Messiah

II

In deciphering letters
that burn on a cold stone
you will explore the language of darkness
and the language of shadows. Motionless
in prayer, like a hunchbacked olivetree,
you will search for keys
lost by God in the wadi of Kidron

III

Formed out of stony earth,
of solitude fencing this town
where the sorrow of the defeated
is a yashmak veiling the faces of women
where candles of life never set
I am digging in time built
into walls beneath walls.

The Citadel and general view of the Old City and Mount of Olives.

Thou art beautiful, O my love,
sweet and comely as Jerusalem:
terrible as an army set in array.
Turn away thy eyes from me,
for they have made me flee away.
Thy hair is as a flock of goats,
that appear from Galaad.
Thy teeth as a flock of sheep,
which come up from the washing, all with
twins,
and there is none barren among them,
Thy cheeks are as the bark of a pomegranate,
beside what is hidden within thee.
There are threescore queens, and fourscore
concubines,
and young maidens without number.
One is my dove, my perfect one is but one,
She is the only one of her mother,
The chosen of her that bore her.
The daughters saw her, and declared her
most blessed:
the queens and concubines, and they
praised her.

Canticle of Canticles 6, 3–8

The church of the Nativity in Bethleem by J. J. Crew.

JERUSALEM
THE IRREPLACEABLE

by Professor Neher

The intertwining of Jerusalem and of the irreplaceable has never been felt by human consciousness with as much obstinate strength and poignant evidence as by the very consciousness that discovered it on the banks of the rivers of Babylon and which, ever since, without respite, pause or parenthesis, has sensed it, sung it, cried out for it throughout the course of history – Jewish consciousness.

Indeed, Christian consciousness very rapidly found another Jerusalem in Rome and in the heavens ; Moslem consciousness too, from the time it came into being, built one in Mecca and Medina ; finally, agnostic consciousness erected still others in Paris, New York and Peking.

Only the Jews, long before there were any Christians, Moslems or believers in a third testament, *would have no other* and have, ever since, with fierce steadfastness, persisted in their refusal to replace Jerusalem, though it be only ruins and dust, by another Jerusalem, though it be heavenly or like Paradise.

We will have no other, cried the Jews during the nights of bitter weeping and in the first light of dawn ; we will have no other, said the Jews, gritting their teeth or with the ghost of a bitter smile, every time that, on the road of their long Exile, they were offered in exchange a final and peaceful stopping place within a Jerusalem other than that which, lying there, on its rock, seemed quite dead and could only present them with the stones of an ageing Wall, the access to which, moreover, would soon be denied them.

I will have no other because, indeed, the Exile has never been to me a fortuitous march without a compass. Never, in the worst of my flights, have I been a wanderer without landmarks. Every step had a meaning : never have I been the Wandering Jew. I have always been the Pilgrim of Jerusalem. Every wandering was oriented towards it. Never have I felt settled anywhere : my prayers, my offerings, my yearnings, and often my steps made me the everlasting Lover of Zion. Every martyrdom was a sacrifice, because the endless dreams of my

Public prayer at the Western Wall.

people brought the humblest, but also the most sorrowful of my ashes to the Mount of Olives.

Thus, Exile itself was a road, the road returning to Jerusalem. And now that this road has brought me back to Jerusalem ; now that its name is Israel and that there it exists, built up, lined with tears, laughter, trees and human-beings as manifold as the millions of irreplaceables – who, while they lived and when they died, had no other name upon their lips but Jerusalem ; now that Jerusalem is not anymore the *symbol* of the irreplaceable but stands for its *reality ;* now, do you believe that I, a Jew, would love another, have another, accept another one ?

« Shma Israel ».

Selected poems essays and other quotations in order of entry, have been contributed by,

WIESEL Elie (1928)
from A Beggar in Jerusalem
published by Random House Inc.
translated from the French
by Lily Edelman and the author   11

MADAULE Jacques (1898)
French writer and historian
Honorary president of the French Association
for Judeo-Christian Friendship
Introduction to this book:
The Unity of Jerusalem
translated from the French by Victoria Sales   12-17

KARNI Yehuda (1884-1948)
Wedge Me into the Fissure
Gladden me, O Jerusalem
translated from the Hebrew by Dom Moraes   20 46

CHATEAUBRIAND, François René de (1768-1848)
Quotations from his journal
Itinerary from Paris to Jerusalem
first published in 1811 translated from the
French by Lida Schechtman-Behrman   23 26-27

RACINE Jean (1636-1699)
Athaliah, act 3, scene 7
translated from the French   24

DONNE John (1573-1631)
The lamentations of Jeremy,
for the most part according to Tremellius,
from Divine Poems   25

HEINE Heinrich (1797-1856)
If, Jerusalem, I Ever Should Forget Thee   29
By the Waters of Babylon   34
Hebrew melodies, translated from the German

AGGADAH
Destruction of the Temple   31

BYRON George Gordon, Lord (1788-1824)
On the Days of the Destruction of Jerusalem by Titus   31

HALEVI Yehuda (1075-1141)
Most Fair of Cities
from *Poems of Zion* translated from the Hebrew   36

HERZL Theodor (1860-1904)
Jerusalem, Diary November 1898
translated from the German by Harry Zohn   40

LAMARTINE Alphonse (1790-1869)
Quotations from his journal
Journey to the Orient
first published in 1834
translated from the French
by Lida Schechtman-Behrman   42 44 88

LENSKI Haim (1905-1942)
Fresh is the Air
translated from the Hebrew by Robert Friend   50

KAMOUN Ali (1929)
Historian of arab palestinian origin
Jerusalem, a Moslem Viewpoint   52

AMICHAI Yehuda (1924)
Jerusalem 1961
translated from the Hebrew by Dennis Silk   56
Jerusalem 1967
translated from the Hebrew by Harold Schimmel   84 98

DANTE Alighieri (1265-1321)
Quotation from the *Divine Comedy*
Purgatory Canto 2
translated from the Italian   60

BIALIK Hayyim Nahman (1873-1934)
Spread your wing
translated from the Hebrew
by Dom Moraes   64
Prophet, Go, Flee!
translated from the Hebrew
by Ruth Finer Mintz (Excerpts)   106
The Talmud Student
translated from the Hebrew
by M. Samuel   114

KAMZON Jacob David (1900)
I Walk in the Holy City
translated from the Hebrew   67

ROKEACH David (1916)
Beginning
Translated from the Hebrew
by Robert Meze   68
Jerusalem 1968
translated from the Hebrew by Alan Brownjohn   124

Father RIQUET Michel S.J. (1899)
Former internee, (World War II), preacher at
Notre-Dame de Paris, is one of the
founder of the French Association
gathering Jews, Christians and Moslems
« The Fraternity of Abraham »
Sacrifice and Reconciliation
translated from the French by Victoria Sales   71-76

Prof. MEHL Roger
Dean of the Protestant Faculty of Theology
at the University of Strasbourg
Symbolic Significance of Jerusalem
A Protestant Viewpoint
translated from the French by Victoria Sales   80-83

ALTERMAN Nathan (1910-1970)
The Olive Tree
translated from the Hebrew by Robert Friend   90
and excerpts from
Hagigat Kayitz
translated from the Hebrew by Dov Vardi   116

RAAB Esther (1899)
Holy Grandmothers in Jerusalem
translated from the Hebrew
by Avraham Birman   92

SHLONSKY Avraham (1900-1973)
Prayer
translated from the Hebrew by Ruth Finer Mintz
(Excerpts)   94

RIMON I.Z. 1889-1958)
God Lives!
translated from the Hebrew by R. Flants   102

GOLDBERG Lea (1911-1970)
Heavenly Jerusalem
Jerusalem of the Earth
translated from the Hebrew
by Robert Friend   104

FICHMAN Yaakov (1881-1958)
Jerusalem
translated from the Hebrew
by Robert Friend   108

SCHNEOUR Zalman (1887-1959)
Welcome Queen Sabbath   111
Song of the Snow   118
translated from the Hebrew by Ruth Finer Mintz

GORDON Judah Leib (1831-1892)
Simhat Torah   113

Prof. NEHER André (1913)
Jerusalem the Irreplaceable
from his book « Dans tes portes Jérusalem »
published by Albin Michel, Paris,
collection Présence du Judaïsme
translated from the French
by Lida Schechtman-Behrman   130-131

Quotations from the Old and New Testament
are from the Holy Bible, in the Westminster text,
under the editorial direction of Father Philip Caraman,
published by Hawthorn Book New York 1958

Quotations from the Koran
have been translated by Muhammad Zafrulla Khan
published by Curzon Press Ltd., London and Dublin (1970)

Translations by D. Moraes, R. Friend, A. Birman and R. Flantz
are taken from the Anthology
of Modern Hebrew Poetry
by the Institute for the Translation of Hebrew Literature

Translations by Ruth Finer Mintz
are taken from her bilingual anthology
Modern Hebrew Poetry
University of California Press (1966-68-75)

IMPRIMÉ EN FRANCE

Imprimerie-Reliure Maison Mame Tours
Dépôt légal : 2e trimestre 1981